Greater Than a Tourist

Reviews

I think the series is wonderful and beneficial for tourists to get information before visiting the city.

-Seckin Zumbul, Izmir Turkey

I am a world traveler who has read many trip guides but this one really made a difference for me. I would call it a heartfelt creation of a local guide expert instead of just a guide.

-Susy, Isla Holbox, Mexico

New to the area like me, this is a must have!

-Joe, Bloomington, USA

This is a good series that gets down to it when looking for things to do at your destination without having to read a novel for just a few ideas.

-Rachel, Monterey, USA

Good information to have to plan my trip to this destination.

-Pennie Farrell, Mexico

Great ideas for a port day.

-Mary Martin USA

Mandy Herrington

Aptly titled, you won't just be a tourist after reading this book. You'll be greater than a tourist!

-Alan Warner, Grand Rapids, USA

Thank you for a fantastic book.

-Don, Philadelphia, USA

Even though I only have three days to spend in San Miguel in an upcoming visit, I will use the author's suggestions to guide some of my time there. An easy read - with chapters named to guide me in directions I want to go.

-Robert Catapano, USA

Great insights from a local perspective! Useful information and a very good value!

-Sarah, USA

This series provides an in-depth experience through the eyes of a local. Reading these series will help you to travel the city in with confidence and it'll make your journey a unique one.

-Andrew Teoh, Ipoh, Malaysia

>TOURIST

GREATER THAN A TOURIST – NORTH YORKSHIRE UNITED KINGDOM

50 Travel Tips from a Local

Mandy Herrington

Mandy Herrington

Greater Than a Tourist- North Yorkshire United Kingdom Copyright © 2018 by CZYK Publishing LLC. All Rights Reserved.

All rights reserved. No part of this book may be reproduced in any form or by any electronic or mechanical means including information storage and retrieval systems, without permission in writing from the author. The only exception is by a reviewer, who may quote short excerpts in a review.

Cover designed by: Lisa Rusczyk Ed. D.
Cover Image: https://pixabay.com/en/england-whitby-robin-hood-s-bay-old-2789824/

Edited by:Linda Fitak

Greater Than a Tourist
Visit our website at www.GreaterThanaTourist.com

Lock Haven, PA
All rights reserved.
I ISBN-13: 978-1717205285

ISBN-10: 1717205283

\>TOURIST

>TOURIST
50 TRAVEL TIPS FROM A LOCAL

Mandy Herrington

BOOK DESCRIPTION

Are you excited about planning your next trip?

Do you want to try something new?

Would you like some guidance from a local?

If you answered yes to any of these questions, then this Greater Than a Tourist book is for you.

Greater Than a Tourist- Greater Than a Tourist- North Yorkshire United Kingdom by Mandy Herrington offers the inside scoop on North Yorkshire. Most travel books tell you how to travel like a tourist. Although there is nothing wrong with that, as part of the Greater Than a Tourist series, this book will give you travel tips from someone who has lived at your next travel destination.

In these pages, you will discover advice that will help you throughout your stay. This book will not tell you exact addresses or store hours but instead will give you excitement and knowledge from a local that you may not find in other smaller print travel books.

Travel like a local. Slow down, stay in one place, and get to know the people and the culture. By the time you finish this book, you will be eager and prepared to travel to your next destination.

Mandy Herrington

\>TOURIST

TABLE OF CONTENTS

BOOK DESCRIPTION
TABLE OF CONTENTS
DEDICATION
ABOUT THE AUTHOR
HOW TO USE THIS BOOK
FROM THE PUBLISHER
OUR STORY
WELCOME TO
\> TOURIST
INTRODUCTION
1. Scarborough Castle
2. Peasholm Park
3. The Open Air Theatre
4. Open Topped Bus
5. Oliver's Mount
6. Tour De Yorkshire- Stage Finish
7. Scarborough Cricket Festival
8. Honda Goldwings Light Parade
9. St Josephs Theatre
10. Scarborough Spa Complex
11. Robin Hoods Bay
12. Whitby
13. Whitby Abbey

Mandy Herrington

14. Whitby Goth Weekend
15. North Yorkshire Moors National Park.
16. The Black Swan Olstead
17. Thirsk
18. North Yorkshire Moor Railways
19. GOATHLAND
20. Pickering War Weekend
21. Playdale Farm
22. Scarborough Footgolf
23. Muston Scarecrow Festival
24. Lebberston Sunday Market
25. Scarborough Fair Collection
26. Filey
27. Filey Museum
28. Filey Bird Garden
29. Spirit of Yorkshire
30. Wolds Way Lavender
31. Malton
32. Thornton-le-Dale
33. Dalby Forest.
34. Pickering
35. Flamingoland
36. Eden Camp
37. Castle Howard
38. Selby
39. Northallerton

>TOURIST

40. Hambleton's markets
41. Ampleforth Abbey
42. Helmsley
43. Catterick Racecourse
44. Richmond
45. Harrogate
46. Theakstons Old Peculiar Crime Festival
47. Great Yorkshire Show
48. Lightwater Valley
49. Skipton
50. Knaresborough

TOP REASONS TO BOOK THIS TRIP
50 THINGS TO KNOW ABOUT PACKING LIGHT FOR TRAVEL
Packing and Planning Tips
NOTES

\>TOURIST

DEDICATION

This book is lovingly dedicated to my parents. Had they not brought me to Scarborough for a fortnight's holiday every year since I was 2 years old, I wouldn't have fallen in love with the whole area and consequently made it my second home.

Mandy Herrington

>TOURIST

ABOUT THE AUTHOR

Mandy Herrington, although born in the city of Durham, has lived almost always in Scarborough since her twenties. Although her travels have been restricted to the UK, she takes every opportunity to get out and about within the whole of Yorkshire. Mandy dreams of visiting the USA one day to see the Grand Canyon and Niagara falls and shop at Macy*s.

Until then, Mandy is content with knitting for her favourite charity projects, reading crime novels, compiling her family tree and developing her spiritual well being.

She has been living here for over 10 years and is very much involved in the annual Armed Forces Day as well as performing in a local amateur pantomime group. The town has seen a lot of change, but it doesn't matter how many times she goes off on an adventure, or visit her family in Durham, seeing the sea and the castle is the sign that she's home.

Mandy Herrington

>TOURIST

HOW TO USE THIS BOOK

The Greater Than a Tourist book series was written by someone who has lived in an area for over three months. The goal of this book is to help travelers either dream or experience different locations by providing opinions from a local. The author has made suggestions based on their own experiences. Please do your own research before traveling to the area in case the suggested places are unavailable.

Mandy Herrington

\>TOURIST

FROM THE PUBLISHER

Traveling can be one of the most important parts of a person's life. The anticipation and memories that you have are some of the best. As a publisher of the Greater Than a Tourist book series, as well as the popular 50 Things to Know book series, we strive to help you learn about new places, spark your imagination, and inspire you. Wherever you are and whatever you do I wish you safe, fun, and inspiring travel.

Lisa Rusczyk Ed. D.
CZYK Publishing

Mandy Herrington

>TOURIST

OUR STORY

Traveling is a passion of the "Greater than a Tourist" series creator. Lisa studied abroad in college, and for their honeymoon Lisa and her husband toured Europe. During her travels to Malta, an older man tried to give her some advice based on his own experience living on the island since he was a young boy. She was not sure if she should talk to the stranger but was interested in his advice. When traveling to some places she was wary to talk to locals because she was afraid that they weren't being genuine. Through her travels, Lisa learned how much locals had to share with tourists. Lisa created the "Greater Than a Tourist" book series to help connect people with locals. A topic that locals are very passionate about sharing.

Mandy Herrington

>TOURIST

WELCOME TO
> TOURIST

Mandy Herrington

>TOURIST

INTRODUCTION

Twenty years from now you will be more disappointed by the things you didn't do than by the ones you did. So throw off the bowlines, sail away from the safe harbour. Catch the trade winds in your sail. Explore. Dream. Discover.

Mark Twain

North Yorkshire is the largest non-metreopolitan county encased within the larger ceremonial county in England. It covers an area of 8,654 square kilometers, taking in part of the Yorkshire Dales National Park, the North Yorkshire Moors National Parks, and part of the Yorkshire Wolds. The two main towns are Scarborough and Harrogate but the county town is the smaller town of Northallerton.

Visitors are well catered for across the region and the amount of things to do outstrips these 50 tips, a thousand times over. There are people who only come

Mandy Herrington

to visit a small area, such as the coast, the towns, hike in the parks, participate in outdoor activities like golf and surfing, or come just for the day out.

I have included as many ideas as possible, places to go and things to do, based on my own experiences. My apologies if your favourite location or activity is not included. All places and activities are easy to research on the internet. Most places are accessible to the disabled, and discounts are available throughout the year, especially if booked in advance. Mobile phone coverage may be intermittent in some of the isolated spots, so please be aware in order to stay safe. The coast is also changeable, so always make sure that you never go off on your own, no matter the excitement.

1. SCARBOROUGH CASTLE

This stunning location is situated on the headland overlooking both bays. It is managed by English Heritage. This is a great day out for the whole family. Explore 3000 years of history, including the bombing by Germans warships on 16th December 1914, and view the stunning panoramic views of the Yorkshire coast. You've got the Sealife Centre to the north; the harbour, Grand hotel and Spa to the south. Sample the wines on offer. I especially like the garden mint and strawberry. There are events going on for the whole family throughout the summer. If you purchase membership of EH you can get onto all their other sites for free.

Later, walk down past the magnificent castle walls towards the restored lighthouse, take a sea journey on the Hispaniola, or the Regal Lady, which was one of the little ships that went to Dunkirk. Have an ice cream float at the Harbour bar and of course, fish and chips. I usually go to the Princess Cafe or The Fish Pan. Just remember not to feed the seagulls.

Mandy Herrington

2. Peasholm Park

This free to walk around oriental themed park is situated on the north side of the town, just off the seafront. It has a central island with a pagoda which is open at times to walk around during the summer season when the attractions are open. Ride around the island on a series of different boats from the new jetty, or sit on the many seats and watch the naval warfare battle, based on the Battle of the River Plate. Usually you can listen to the organ music for free. As you walk through the park, you can see a wide variety of trees, including the previously believed extinct Dicksonian Elm. Pop a coin in the wishing well, or visit the secret garden. Round off your visit with a game of minature golf. Refreshments are usually just available during the summer season and toilets for the disabled are just outside the park near the seafront.

3. THE OPEN AIR THEATRE

Beside Peasholm park is Northstead Manor Gardens park. Here you will find the largest open air theatre in Europe, situated on an island, facing a 6500 seated amphitheatre reopened in 2010, by the Queen. Elton John was the first of many acts to have since played here during its summer season, including my favourite group Status Quo. This winter they have covered the lake to make a standing area. There is a small area especially for those in wheelchairs, but it must be booked in advance. Parking is limited, on a first come basis. Also in the park is the North Bay Miniature Railway and the water chute. I don't care how old I am, I do so love riding on these!

4. OPEN TOPPED BUS

Take a trip round Marine Drive from The Sands to the Spa and back again if you so wish, on one of the open topped buses, that is in operation during the summer months. You'd best have a coat on when on the top deck, as it gets a bit cold, if the wind is really gusty. Wave at Fred on his seat opposite the Oasis cafe, look up at the imposing headland, where the seagulls nest above the skate park, pass the harbour, all the amusements and shops to reach the Victorian Spa and entertainment complex. Ticket offers are usually available but I usually walk round from the Spa and bus back.

Mandy Herrington

5. OLIVER'S MOUNT

This is the highest point from which to see the whole of Scarborough. There is no bus to this location so you need a vehicle or walk. You can reach it from behind the Mere on Seamer Road or the turning on Filey Road. It has been one of the hill climbs in the Tour de Yorkshire. In summer, there are motor cycle road races. There is a cafe with disabled access and on a weekend, local football teams play on the pitches. The town's war memorial is situated here, and there is a service every Remembrance Sunday, when there is a bus. I always wrap up in layers when I go on Remembrance Sunday to pay my respects to the soldiers who gave their lives in conflicts since 1945.

6. TOUR DE YORKSHIRE- STAGE FINISH

Following Yorkshire's successful Grand Départ in the first stage of the Tour de France 2014, Yorkshire has gone on to stage its own 3 day annual event encompassing the whole of the Yorkshire region.

Scarborough has been a stage finish at every Tour de Yorkshire event since its inauguration event in 2015. This televised event is so popular that it is expanded to four days. The iconic finish sees the cyclists race round the Aquarium top roundabout, along the seafront, over the cobble paving to sprint to the finish on Marine Drive, as we call it. There is a family fun party event at the finish line for most of the day. I usually stand somewhere on the foreshore and cheer them on the last couple of kilometers.

7. SCARBOROUGH CRICKET FESTIVAL

Throughout the summer you can always hear leather on willow at the North Marine Road cricket ground, finishing with a two week festival in August. Yorkshire Cricket Club usually plays one or two county matches here during the 2nd half of their season. This is such a popular event within the cricket itinerary, that tickets go fast, so it is best to book early to get discounts. Children and people with disabilities are welcomed, and there are wheelchair friendly viewing sites. Over the years, I have spent many a happy time, seeing lots of well known stars and teams, marking the runs off in my program, eating chicken and watching the ball being hit out of the ground. My dad always claims that I had my photograph taken with Sir Garfield Sobers at this ground when I was a child. No proof though.

8. HONDA GOLDWINGS LIGHT PARADE

This is an annual day long event that occurs in September and gains in popularity every year. Honda Goldwing motorbikes and trikes descend on the town, park up on West pier and the Foreshore. Residents and tourists alike can view them. The bikers spend the day collecting for that year's charity and some give rides, but avoid getting fingerprints on their bikes before they are judged. The winning bike leads the parade. When it gets dark, they dress up their bikes with fairy lights and at the designated hour, switch them on and parade along the foreshore to the Aquarium top roundabout, back and along marine drive, then back to the pier. This is followed by a fireworks display. I can't miss this out, as I am one of the volunteer helpers stewarding the event, keeping people off the road as the bikes pass and stand on the beach, cordoning off the fireworks area while the fireworks are released to music.

9. ST JOSEPHS THEATRE

This is a unique venue, due to its round theatre. It also contains the standard McCarthy auditorium as well. Long standing artistic director and playwright is Alan Ayckbourn, and his plays are usually performed here. This theatre is considered one of the most renowned in the country. The theatre complex is disabled friendly, and there is an audio loop, as well as special audio and sign language performances. It is advisable to pre-book, as they are popular. There is a small restaurant where you can have a meal, pre-show drinks or sometimes see a performance by one of the outreach script writing groups. Tickets vary in price and you can block book for several shows at a discount. I like to go and support local playwrights when they showcase their work, as they are people I know.

10. SCARBOROUGH SPA COMPLEX

This is a Grade II listed venue, originally built around the source of the Scarborough spa waters. Max Jaffa, violinist and band leader, played here in the summer and you can still listen to an orchestra in the Suncourt. Be entertained in the 600 seat Victorian theatre with a summer show or pantomime. In the Grand Hall, you'll find various musical acts, including a jazz festival and Northern soul performances. There are also events such as sci fi weekend, vintage fair and tattoo shows. Have a meal and drink in the cafe or Farrer's restaurant, or visit the shops nearby. Take a tram ride up the 200ft cliff, or walk up through the Italian gardens behind the complex to the clock tower at the top. This iconic symbol was in the television series The Royal.

11. ROBIN HOODS BAY

Jump aboard the hourly Arriva 93/93X service to Middlesborough, and stop off at Robin Hoods Bay on route to Whitby. This small fishing village and bay used to be the heart of all smuggling operations in the area. Legend has it that there is a subterranean network of passageways linking houses together underneath the twisting streets and alleyways. Walk the railway track or part of the Cleveland Way to Whitby, or walk along the beach in the other direction. This is a good place to find fossils, as this area is known as being part of the Dinosaur coast. Stop at Boggle Hole Youth Hostel. This was my first ever YHA experience and I stayed here with my schoolmates when I was in my teens.

12. WHITBY

Whitby is a port on the river Esk, surrounded by the National park, but it is not actually included within it. The river dissects the two sides of the town. Whitby has links to whaling with the Whale bone arch situated on West cliff above the Spa pavillion as well as being the place where Captain Cook (1746-1755) started out in his naval career. The house he lodged in is now a museum. The town is also famous for its Whitby jet jewellery, made popular by Queen Victoria in her mourning period. There is also a wide range of quirky shops, Fortunes, cafes and restaurants. I always visit the Magpie and then take a walk along the pier. Whitby has appeared quite frequently in episodes of Heartbeat and the Royal.

13. WHITBY ABBEY

Managed by English Heritage, the historic Gothic Abbey ruins dominate the skyline, where you can get some stunning panoramic views of the town. Along with the town's seafaring past, it was the inspiration for the novel Dracula by Bram Stoker. There are several Dracula inspired events around the town including the Dracula experience and a walk which starts at the whalebone arch in an evening. The abbey is most alive during Halloween, although they have events throughout the year for the whole family. Discounts are available and there is parking nearby. A popular tradition is to climb the 199 steps to reach the abbey. If the steps appear daunting, then follow the smell of oak smoke to Fortunes to buy smoked kippers. They are awesome.

14. WHITBY GOTH WEEKEND

This is a twice yearly music festival for goths which starts on a Friday morning and runs till a Sunday. It was chosen as the venue, due to its Dracula connections. The Halloween weekend event is extremely popular attracting large numbers of non goths who love to dress up in costume. You can buy whole weekend or daily tickets, and you need to book your accommodation early as it soon gets booked up. First timers are known as goth virgins and are encouraged to meet at the Spa Pavillion on a Friday morning for an induction. Also during the Halloween event is the Bram Stoker film festival.

15. NORTH YORKSHIRE MOORS NATIONAL PARK.

This is one of two National parks within the area. The other is Yorkshire Dales, of which only a section lies within the county border. This park is 1,430 square km, and covers the North Sea coastline inland towards the Cleveland Hills and the Vale of Pickering (boundaries). Most of its rocks date back to the Jurassic period, and the coastline is known as the Dinosaur Coast. Examples can be found in the Rotunda Museum in Scarborough. The park has is perfect for walking, cycling and touring. Its lovely nature reserves and trails, such as Cleveland Way, are perfect for exploring. There are many camping and caravan parks for your stay, as well as B&Bs, cottages and hotels. And always follow the country code: let people know your route, as phone signals are unreliable in some of the more isolated places. You don't want the Yorkshire Air Ambulance or mountain rescue volunteers to have to come and rescue you.

Mandy Herrington

16. THE BLACK SWAN OLSTEAD

Located on the edge of the moors, 20 miles north of York and 6 miles from A19 in the city of Olstead, you will find the Black Swan Pub. Run by Michelin Star Chef and winner of Great British Menu 2016 and 2017, Tommy Banks and his family, they produce traditional Yorkshire Fayre with a mix of creativity and eccentricity from produce sourced locally and grown in their own gardens. They offer adult only accommodation and a taster menu but it must be pre-booked. Children over 12 can eat in the restaurant, but there are no facilities for younger children. Diets can be catered for, but must be arranged in advance, due to ingredients. You need your own transport to access this location, as there is no local taxi service.

17. THIRSK

This small market town is situated near the centre of the county. Cricket fans must visit the Thirsk Museum, birthplace of Thomas Lord, who founded Lord's Cricket Ground in London. Horse racing fans traipse to the racecourse for one of the 16 days flat racing, finishing off the season with Ladies day. The Ritz cinema is a 200 seater run by volunteers, and is considered one of the oldest cinemas in the UK still operating. The most well known resident was James Alfred Wight also known as the author James Herriot (died 1995). Discover the World of James Herriot Museum, opened in 1999, and popularised in the Television series "All Creatures Great and Small." The social history museum depicts veterinary rural life in the 1940s. Wheelchairs can access all areas, except the air raid shelter. This is a great day out for the whole family! If you still want more, then go out and explore the surrounding area known as Herriot country.

18. NORTH YORKSHIRE MOOR RAILWAYS

If you want an amazing scenic journey soaked in the history of steam or diesel, then head for Whitby station and jump aboard the NYMR, as seen on TV. This 24 mile railway is run by volunteers and you can board and jump off at any station on route. At Grosmont, walk through the George Stephenson tunnel and visit the engine workshops. This busy station is the junction not only of the heritage line, but also links the mainline to the Esk Valley line. At

Mandy Herrington

Goathland you must get your picture taken on the Hogwarts school platform at Levisham, and see the NYMR artist in residence. Finally, get off at Pickering and see its 1930s themed station. Follow the colour-coded timetable to plan your visit, as there are also special events throughout the year. Pre-booking is helpful if you require wheelchair access. Alternatively, go in the opposite direction and end up in Whitby. A fun day out for the whole family!

19. GOATHLAND

This popular village is accessible all year round, although if you want the Heartbeat experience only, then the summer is best time to go. Get your photo taken outside Scripp's garage, have a picnic on the three quarter mile long village green, surrounded by wandering sheep. Say 'cheers' while having a pint in the Aidensfield Arms, and of course, buy some souvenirs at the local shop. Outside the village, there are 9 waterfalls to find in the surrounding valleys. It can be reached by car on the NYMR route, and parking is available. You could also take the 840 Leeds to Whitby Coastliner. This is no more than a two hour visit, unless you plan to go out into the surrounding countryside.

20. PICKERING WAR WEEKEND

This October three day extravaganza is organised by the North Yorkshire Moors Railway, and it is a series of WW2 and 1940s themed events, originally based around its stations. It has become so popular that it has spilled out into Pickering itself, and has exploded into an event that must be on everyone's calendar. There is always singing and dancing, workshops for the whole family, parades, vehicles, and re-enactments. The final event is a parade down Pickering Main St. Every station has its own theme, with special activities. There is something for everyone. Do keep your children close to you at all times, as there can be throngs of over 20 thousand visitors per day. Plan ahead of time where to meet, in case you get separated. I like seeing all the different outfits that people wear and having a good old sing song.

21. PLAYDALE FARM

Jump aboard the EYMS 120/121 bus to Hull, and stop off in Cayton. Along a well-worn and beaten track is the farm, which can be enjoyed by the whole family. Feed the animals, then go for a ride on the go carts or zip line. There are indoor and outdoor play areas, so playtime does not stop if it rains. Try your hand at frisbee golf… I did, and it is not as easy as it looks, believe you me! There are many hand washing facilities and reminders to wash your hands. There is a cafe and gift shop, and many places for picnics. Group visits are encouraged and discounts are available.

22. SCARBOROUGH FOOTGOLF

Not far away from Playdale farm, next to the stained glass centre, there is a nine hole golf course that you play with a size 5 football. No need for any fancy equipment and football boots are banned. In fact, you only need to wear your trainers and you can even bring your own football. If footgolf is too strenuous for you, try their footpool. These activities are suitable for the whole family, even for fitness challenged people like me. It can be a bit expensive for individual admission, but discounts are given for larger groups. You book for a time slot, so it is advisable to pre-book, as some slots are more popular than others. You also need to turn up on time, to keep your slot! Discounts are available. Look out for crazy footgolf coming soon!

23. MUSTON SCARECROW FESTIVAL

Muston village is situated 2 miles from Filey on the Yorkshire Wold Way National Trail. This week-long event began in 1999, and has grown to world wide attention. Local residents construct scarecrows depicting famous people and celebrities, and display them in their gardens and other locations around the village. Sheets are available depicting the entries, so walk round the village trying to find them. And for added fun, vote for your favourite. They also do themes, such as the London Olympics. A farmer provides a uneven field for paid car parking, and refreshments are made available in the local village hall, church and pub. Coaches may drop off passengers in the village, but must park outside the village. It is a nice quirky day out.

Mandy Herrington

24. LEBBERSTON SUNDAY MARKET

This is one place I go fortnightly. It is the local Sunday market and car boot venue located just outside Filey. It is only open between Easter and September, but is well attended by locals and holiday makers from the nearby holiday parks. Although I go on the 120/121 EYMS bus, there is ample free car parking in the field next door. It has regular stalls alongside food outlets, a few rides a bouncy castle and of course, the car booters where you can get some real gems. If you want to make some money, bring your old knick knacks and sell them. For me, I go elephant and owl hunting, grab some fresh fruit and of course, chocolate.

25. SCARBOROUGH FAIR COLLECTION

Situated in the grounds of the Flower of May holiday park at Lebberston is this collection, one of the hidden gems on the coast. See steam traction engines from the past, including the one from The Iron Maiden film, 1962. Take a nostalgic fairground ride, or listen to the mechanical organs. Smell the aroma of the vintage cars, motor bikes and other vehicles. There is something for everyone, whatever your age. You can even attend tea dances and tango to the organ music of bygone years. Some of these items are part of a travelling exhibit, so they are out and about the country for everyone's pleasure. It is advisable to check the website for opening days. Cars can park on site and the 120/121 stops at the main entrance to the park, so be prepared for a bit of a walk.

26. FILEY

Filey Town is a small seaside resort, surrounded by holiday parks. It is split into the old historic side and the modern tourist venue. The Scarborough to Hull train stops here. There is a wide range of shops, cafes and restaurants, catering for every taste. Facilities vary, depending on the time of year. You can walk to the top, towards the children's play park, then down onto the promenade, where you will reach the local lifeboat station. This is one of many found on the coastline, manned by volunteers 24/7. Keep walking along to reach the 12th Century St. Oswald's Church. I always make this trip by train.

Mandy Herrington

27. FILEY MUSEUM

Wander over the bridge from St. Oswald's church, past some fishing cottages, and you will come across this tiny museum. It is two houses, a converted fisherman's and farm cottage that have merged and have been given grade 2 listed status. Within this museum of seven rooms and small outdoor area, discover Filey's immense past, from its fishing roots to its development into a holiday resort and the distinction of having the first Butlin's holiday park located on its outskirts. I learnt that fisherman's jumpers had meanings, depending on the cable pattern used to knit them. The museum has won awards as best small visitor attraction, and prides itself on its disabled facilities and guided tours. It is well worth the admission fee.

28. FILEY BIRD GARDEN

This hidden treasure is situated about a mile from Filey town centre on the outskirts. Discover the wide range of small animals that live there. You can also feed them. View the exotic birds and admire the beautiful gardens, which include a sensory garden for the visually impaired. Also discover their secret garden! There is a play area where you can view the countryside around for miles. This small 5 acre park promises to satisfy every family member, and it is dog friendly. Car parking is free and the 120/121 bus stops nearby. I can't wait to go back when the wallabies arrive!

29. SPIRIT OF YORKSHIRE

Situated close to the train station in Hunmanby on the industrial estate is Yorkshire's first single malt distillery. They offer samples of the latest releases to everyone on their one hour introductory tour, led by one of the actual distillers. If you don't like whiskey, you can still enjoy refreshments in the Pot Still Coffee Shop, open to the general public. There are also premium tours and masterclasses available. It is advisable to pre-book, due to tour times, and to ensure that you are guaranteed your place. The distillery is open seven days a week and under 18s can enjoy the tour, if accompanied by an adult, although they won't get any whiskey. Finish your visit off with a trip to the shop, where there is a selection of whiskies to purchase.

Mandy Herrington

30. WOLDS WAY LAVENDER

This unique family run farm is situated near the A64. The farm is dedicated to the growing, distilling and selling of lavender goods. It is a great day out for the whole family, including the dog. Wander about and inhale the heady varied lavender fragrances, as you walk among the wild flowers and various sculptures. Everyone can ride on the train, when it is in operation, and if you visit at the right time of year, you can actually see the lavender oil being distilled. Compete with family members in the giant games, walk the nature trail or even enjoy a lavender scone in the tearoom. Buy a plant to take home. If you visit twice, your third visit is free!

31. MALTON

This is North Yorkshire's food capital. This traditional market town has reinvented itself as the place to go for food, and visitors will be enthralled with everything: the Talbot Yard food court, the restaurants and cafes and of course, Malton's cookery school. A Yorkshire curd tart is a must for any visitor.

Charles Dickens wrote a Christmas Carol here on one of his visits, so there are Dickens related festivals here, as well as food and drink events throughout the year. Hve a taste of one of the delicoius gelattos on offer! Malton is the halfway mark on the Scarborough to York train line, as well as a stop on the Leeds to Scarborough White Rose Way walk.

32. THORNTON-LE-DALE

This picturesque village is located within the National Park and needs more than just a day to explore. One of its thatched cottages is known as the chocolate box house, as it has appeared on numerous calendars and chocolate boxes over the years. Situated beside the babbling brook is the tiny triangular village green, complete with the old market cross and stocks from its medieval days. The motor museum has an excellent collection of cars and bikes from 1918 to 1976, and a working restoration workshop with a viewing area. If you have a vehicle restoration project, these guys may be able to help. Pick up a copy of their walks or cycling routes and explore the area. There are events throughout the year, including an Annual show, pop-up market,, and the ice cream shop is a must. This is my favourite place outside Scarborough.

33. DALBY FOREST.

Situated near Pickering and Thornton-le dale is a span of 8000 acres of woodland called the Dalby forest, managed by the forestry commission. There are miles of fully accessible trails to walk or cycle, with bicycles, wheelchairs and buggies available to hire. Information, maps, snacks and a children's play area can be found at the visitor centre. There is a full program of events throughout the year, including music festivals and Trackrod motor rally. Wooden forest lodges are available to stay in, and even the Go Ape adventure is situated here. If you're adventurous, and you don't mind heights, you can transverse the valley on zip wires. Or if you're like me, and not very keen on heights, then take a segway ride through the forest.

This is perfect for a family day out, but it is also a huge forest, so do follow the country code.

34. PICKERING

This ancient market town is an ideal place to base yourself, if you want to explore this part of the region. It includes a great amount of small chocolate box villages, stunning countryside and nearby park and POW camp. This small town is the hub for performing arts in the area, with three theatre spaces and an evening ghost walk. Explore the range of shops, and cafes, including the indoor flea market. Also visit Pickering Castle, managed by the English Heritage. In this area, you will find Rosedale abbey with its glass studio, Beck Isle and Ryedale Folk museums, where you can take in the history of the area. In the surrounding countryside, there are ample walking and cycling routes, as well as a trout fishing lake.

35. FLAMINGOLAND

Situated near Pickering is the Flamingoland Zoo and theme park with over 140 species of mammals, reptiles and birds, 8 extreme rides and many smaller rides. Meet Peter Rabbit in the Children's Planet area, take in the pirate shows, and eat from a variety of food outlets, including Coach house, Jolly Sailor, Pizza Pie, plus kiosks too numerous to mention.

Mandy Herrington

"Meet a meerkat" or "be a zookeeper for the day" are some of the extra activities on offer. Book your accommodations in the area to sample even more aspects of the park, including the leisure complex, club entertainment, as well as unrestricted admission to the park. Discounts are available online and the park is totally children and dog friendly, with accommodations for the disabled.

36. EDEN CAMP

This modern history museum, established in 1987, is a great day out for the whole family, including the dog. Set in the grounds and buildings of a WW2 prisoner of war camp, it has been developed to bring British military and social history to life, from 1914 to the present. Each barrack is themed, and I especially found the true-to-life Blitz rather surreal. There are picnic areas, a gift shop and cafe, and the Garrison cinema bar where you can sample the locally brewed Eden Camp bitter. Remember the Dig for Victory slogan? They even have a garden based on this. Parking is free but you need at least 4 hours for your visit. Near to York there is also the Yorkshire Air Museum.

37. CASTLE HOWARD

One of the finest Historic Stately Homes in Britain, it has been owned by the Howard family for generations. Brideshead Revisited, Death Comes to Pemberley and Victoria have all been filmed here. Located 15 miles from York, it is easily accessible by car, and you can get a bus from York direct also. Explore the the 1000 acres of parkland, beautiful gardens and sculptures, and walled garden. Children can enjoy the playground. They have a huge range of events year-round. Admission to the house is extra but you can become a member of Castle Howard, offering you further benefits. Members of the Historic House Association receive one free visit a year. You could also stay on the estate in one of their cottages, or on their camp and caravan site, and explore the surrounding the Howardian Hills!

38. SELBY

Situated south of York, it's easy to forget that this little sector is actually a part of North Yorkshire. This historic market town is mainly rooted in its industrial past. Although located inland from the coast, it was a major shipbuilding port, and a center for coal mining and railways industry. It is now involved in power generation. Hidden heritage leaflets encourage visitors to stroll through its rich history. You can also walk the Trans Pennine trail, which runs from Selby to Hornsea. Selby Abbey's stained glass window is supposedly linked to the family of George Washington as the inspiration for the stars and stripes depicted in the flag. Market day is Monday. As the daughter of a miner, I am always interested in my mining heritage.

39. NORTHALLERTON

This market town is the capital of the county. Situated north of York on the East Coast main line, it is the administrative centre for North Yorkshire County Council, responsible for the districts of Craven, Hambleton, Harrogate, Richmondshire, Ryedale, Scarborough and Selby. It is a great place to base yourself to explore both the moors and dales national parks, as well as Boltby tracking centre. Try your hand at gliding or even visit the Forbidden Corner. In the town, there is a long High Street with a variety of well known shops, alongside pubs, cafes and restaurants and of course Kidzplay. As an avid family history researcher, I love this repository for most of the area's records. It is a must for any fellow historian.

40. HAMBLETON'S MARKETS

Hambleton district is the home of the pretty towns of Bedale, Easingwold, Northallerton, Stokesley and Thirsk, each with their own bustling local market. These markets can be traced back as far back as 1066. Easingwold is the baby - it has been trading for a scant 400 years. There is a market in one of these towns most days, where you can pick up quality food, bargains or whatever you wish. I've only been to Northallerton and Thirsks, but if they were all closer, I would visit every single one of them, including the monthly farmers markets at Easingwold and Stokesley.

41. AMPLEFORTH ABBEY

This thriving monastry, with over 70 Benedictine monks, is also one of the main co-educational catholic boarding schools in the country. In addition to teaching, the monks grow a range of about 40 types of apples in their orchards, used to make apple juice, ciders and cider brandy. Ampleforth Abbey Ale is also brewed. Visitors are always welcome to explore the magnificent church and its grounds. There is a cafe for refreshments and a gift shop to purchase jams, books and religious artifacts. The school section is off limits to all visitors. I was there last Christmas for a carol service, and was surprised to find that their Christmas tree does not go up until Christmas Eve, whereas mine goes up about the start of Advent.

42. HELMSLEY

Helmsley market town, named in the Domesday Book, is what I consider a door. It's where the North Yorkshire Moors National Park meets the Howardian hills, the Cleveland Way meets the Ebor and Inn Way (a trail of public houses), also where the valleys of Bilsdale and Ryedale meet the flat vale of Pickering. Within the town itself are over 50 listed buildings, including the English Heritage managed Helmsley Castle, Birds of Prey centre, open 7 days a week, and over 50 independent and specialist shops. I watched some Whitby jet stone being made into earrings and bought some unusual Christmas presents. There are plenty of tea rooms and the arts centre is well worth a visit. Stay over and explore the area some more.

43. CATTERICK RACECOURSE

This small and compact venue makes it so easy to get up close to the action. There are 27 race days a year, with both flat and jump meets. Admission prices are excellent, and under 18 are admitted free with an accompanying adult. The staff are very helpful, especially helping first-timers pick a winner...or loser in my case, and parking is free. A great day out for the whole family, including the dog. If you enjoy your visit, pop back on a Sunday when the course becomes a very large Sunday market, well attended by residents of Catterick village and the nearby garrison. There are other events throughout the year also.

44. RICHMOND

Situated on the edge of the Yorkshire Dales, this town is steeped in history. Richmond Castle, the Richmondshire Museum and of course the Georgian Theatre Royal, lovingly restored and considered one of Britain's best theatres. Keeping up with its local military connection of the nearby Catterick garrison, is the Green Howard's Regimental Museum, which is now part of the Yorkshire Infantry regiment. My children's granddad served in this regiment in 1971, and was tragically killed during combat. Henry Greathead, the inventor of the lifeboat was born here, and Woman of Substance was filmed here, as well as Reeves and Mortimer's comedy series Catterick. And for those of you who crave a little something other than historical facts: The Station food film and arts centre is very popular with tourists, as its cinemas have a cheese maker and micro brewery!

45. HARROGATE

This Victorian spa town is well known on the international stage for hosting the Eurovision song contest in 1982 and being the first stage finish line of the Tour de France 2014. The Royal Hall Theatre is the only surviving kursaal in Britain, and the Royal Pump Room Museum explains the history of the town's spa. The Royal Horticultural Society manages the only north location of Harlow Carr gardens. Within it is the famous Betty's second tea room, the first being in the market place. Betty's family makes Yorkshire Tea. There are many beautiful parks dotted around the town, including Valley gardens where lots of activities for children are located. For those of you who prefer to be more active, visit the indoor climbing centre.

46. THEAKSTONS OLD PECULIAR CRIME FESTIVAL

This is Europe's largest event dedicated to the celebration of crime fiction. It started in the Old Swan Hotel...as any Agatha Christie Fan knows ... which was where she was found after an absence of 11 days. This has grown over 15 years to be one of the Uk's top literary festivals. This three day event pulls in all authors around the world, and the highlight is the Old Peculiar crime novel of the year award. Accommodation gets booked up very quickly, so reserve in advance of your arrival. The weekend rover ticket is the best option, as you can access most of the festival events. As an aspiring crime novelist, this is always on my annual visits. There are other literary festivals across the county, including Books by the beach, which is in Scarborough.

Mandy Herrington

47. GREAT YORKSHIRE SHOW

This iconic three day agricultural show is now in its 160th year. It is the biggest event in the English calendar and is televised to the nation. Over 8500 animals compete in a wide variety of categories, from cattle and horses to family pets. There are demonstrations of cookery, rural crafts and competitions to enter. Children love to play in the Discovery Zone. Group discounts and advanced tickets are available and further discounts are available with some train tickets. Free shuttle buses bring you from the station to the showground. If you become a member of the Yorkshire Agricultural Society, admission is free. It is very crowded, so ensure you have plans in place in case you get separated from your children or other members of your party.

48. LIGHTWATER VALLEY

Situated outside of Ripon, its slogan is The Ultimate Adventure, and for good reason. It is considered one of the greatest theme parks in the country. It is known for having the longest roller coaster in Europe. It has about 40 rides, classifed by age groups. There is something for the whole family to enjoy, offering indoor and outdoor play, and of course, the Lightwater Express train. There are animal encounters during school holidays and on weekends, adventure golf as well as plenty of food outlets to satisfy all needs. You can take the train to Thirsk, Leeds or Harrogate and then take a bus, or just drive there, as parking is free. Book in advance for discounts. Tickets are purchased according to height.

49. SKIPTON

This market town is situated within the district of Craven, on the edge of the Yorkshire Dales National Park. The Leeds to Liverpool canal passes directly through the centre of the town so there is ample opportunity to enjoy a boat ride, learn the history of

Mandy Herrington

the canal or just sit and watch the world go by. Also, visit the 900 year old beautifully preserved medieval castle and grounds, or venture into the countryside to explore other famous landmarks, such as Bolton Abbey. Skipton has a wonderful market which operates alongside the array of high street shops, the shopping centre, cafes and restaurants. Visit the museum and gallery, and the local parks. There is even an off the road landrover experience to try.

50. KNARESBOROUGH

This historic market and spa town is situated 4 miles east of Harrogate. Its most famous landmark is Mother Shipton's Cave, the oldest attraction in England, open since 1630. It's only a few minutes from the train station. Parking is available in the royal park. Discover the story of the prophetess and be mesmerised by the petrifying wall. Dogs are welcome. However, there is no wheelchair access within the cave, and parts of the park are difficult for mobility impaired people, so it is advisible to seek advice before travelling to avoid disappointment. The park is beautiful to walk through, have a picnic and children have two play areas to enjoy. Nearby is Knaresborough castle.

TOP REASONS TO BOOK THIS TRIP

Coastline: The views are absolutely stunning and the beaches are great.

Food: Traditional Yorkshire pudding and gravy is a must to tickle your taste buds.

Culture: Every town and village has its own unique character, personality and traditions.

Mandy Herrington

Bonus Book

50 THINGS TO KNOW ABOUT PACKING LIGHT FOR TRAVEL

Pack the Right Way Every Time

Author: Manidipa Bhattacharyya

Mandy Herrington

First Published in 2015 by Dr. Lisa Rusczyk. Copyright 2015. All Rights Reserved. No part of this publication may be reproduced, including scanning and photocopying, or distributed in any form or by any means, electronic or mechanical, or stored in a database or retrieval system without prior written permission from the publisher.

Disclaimer: The publisher has put forth an effort in preparing and arranging this book. The information provided herein by the author is provided "as is". Use this information at your own risk. The publisher is not a licensed doctor. Consult your doctor before engaging in any medical activities. The publisher and author disclaim any liabilities for any loss of profit or commercial or personal damages resulting from the information contained in this book.

Edited by Melanie Howthorne

Introduction

*He who would travel happily
must travel light.*

-Antoine de Saint-Exupéry

Travel takes you to different places from seas and mountains to deserts and much more. In your travels you get to interact with different people and their cultures. You will, however, enjoy the sights and interact positively with these new people even more, if you are travelling light.

When you travel light your mind can be free from worry about your belongings. You do not have to spend precious vacation time waiting for your luggage to arrive after a long flight. There is be no chance of your bags going missing and the best part is that you need not pay a fee for checked baggage.

People who have mastered this art of packing light will root for you to take only one carry-on, wherever you go. However, many people can find it really hard to pack light. More so if you are travelling with children. Differentiating between "must have" and "just in case" items is the starting point. There will be ample shopping avenues at your destination which are just waiting to be explored.

Mandy Herrington

This book will show you 'packing' in a new 'light' – pun intended – and help you to embrace light packing practices for all of your future travels.

Off to packing!

Dedication

I dedicate this book to all the travel buffs that I know, who have given me great insights into the contents of their backpacks.

About The Author

Manidipa Bhattacharyya is a creative writer and editor, with an education in English literature and Linguistics. After working in the IT industry for seven long years she decided to call it quits and follow her heart instead. Manidipa has been ghost writing, editing, proof reading and doing secondary research services for many story tellers and article writers for about three years. She stays in Kolkata, India with her husband and a busy two year old. In her own time Manidipa enjoys travelling, photography and writing flash fiction.

Manidipa believes in travelling light and never carries anything that she couldn't haul herself on a trip. However, travelling with her child changed the scenario. She seemed to carry the entire world with her for the baby on the first two trips. But good sense prevailed and she is again working her way to becoming a light traveler, this time with a kid.

Mandy Herrington

The Right Travel Gear

1. Choose Your Travel Gear Carefully

While selecting your travel gear, pick items that are light weight, durable and most importantly, easy to carry. There are cases with wheels so you can drag them along – these are usually on the heavy side because of the trolley. Alternatively a backpack that you can carry comfortably on your back, or even a duffel bag that you can carry easily by hand or sling across your body are also great options. Whatever you choose, one thing to keep in mind is that the luggage itself should not weigh a ton, this will give you the flexibility to bring along one extra pair of shoes if you so desire.

2. Carry The Minimum Number Of Bags

Selecting light weight luggage is not everything. You need to restrict the number of bags you carry as well. One carry-on size bag is ideal for light travel. Most carriers allow one cabin baggage plus one purse, handbag or camera bag as long as it slides under the seat in front. So technically, you can carry two items of luggage without checking them in.

3. Pack One Extra Bag

Always pack one extra empty bag along with your essential items. This could be a very light weight duffel bag or even a sturdy tote bag which takes up minimal space. In the event that you end up buying a lot of souvenirs, you already have a handy bag to stuff all that into and do not have to spend time hunting for an appropriate bag.

> *I'm very strict with my packing and have everything in its right place. I never change a rule. I hardly use anything in the hotel room. I wheel my own wardrobe in and that's it.*
>
> Charlie Watts

Clothes & Accessories

4. Plan Ahead

Figure out in advance what you plan to do on your trip. That will help you to pick that one dress you need for the occasion. If you are going to attend a wedding then you have to carry formal wear. If not, you can ditch the gown for something lighter that will be comfortable during long walks or on the beach.

5. Wear That Jacket

Remember that wearing items will not add extra luggage for your air travel. So wear that bulky jacket that you plan to carry for your trip. This saves space and can also help keep you warm during the chilly flight.

6. Mix and Match

Carry clothes that can be interchangeably used to reinvent your look. Find one top that goes well with a couple of pairs of pants or skirts. Use tops, shirts and jackets wisely along with other accessories like a scarf or a stole to create a new look.

7. Choose Your Fabric Wisely

Stuffing clothes in cramped bags definitely takes its toll which results in wrinkles. It is best to carry wrinkle free, synthetic clothes or merino tops. This will eliminate the need for that small iron you usually bring along.

8. Ditch Clothes Pack Underwear

Pack more underwear and socks. These are the things that will give you a fresh feel even if you do not get a chance to wear fresh clothes. Moreover these are easy to wash and can be dried inside the hotel room itself.

9. Choose Dark Over Light

While picking your clothes choose dark coloured ones. They are easy to colour coordinate and can last longer before needing a wash. Accidental food spills and dirt from the road are less visible on darker clothes.

10. Wear Your Jeans

Take only one pair of Jeans with you, which you should wear on the flight. Remember to pick a pair that can be worn for sightseeing trips and is equally eloquent for dinner. You can add variety by adding light weight cargoes and chinos.

11. Carry Smart Accessories

The right accessory can give you a fresh look even with the same old dress. An intelligent neck-piece, a couple of bright scarves, stoles or a sarong can be used in a number of ways to add variety to your clothing. These light weight beauties can double up as a nursing cover, a light blanket, beach wear, a modesty cover for visiting places of worship, and also makes for an enthralling game of peek-a-boo.

12. Learn To Fold Your Garments

Seasoned travellers all swear by rolling their clothes for compact and wrinkle free packing. Bundle packing, where you roll the clothes around a central object as if tying it up, is also a popular method of compact and wrinkle free packing. Stacking folded clothes one on top of another is a big no-no as it makes creases extreme and they are difficult to get rid of without ironing.

13. Wash Your Dirty Laundry

One of the ways to avoid carrying loads of clothes is to wash the clothes you carry. At some places you might get to use the laundry services or a Laundromat but if you are in a pinch, best solution is to wash them yourself. If that is the plan then carrying quick drying clothes is highly recommended, which most often also happen to be the wrinkle free variety.

14. Leave Those Towels Behind

Regular towels take up a lot of space, are heavy and take ages to dry out. If you are staying at hotels they will provide you with towels anyway. If you are travelling to a remote place, where the availability of towels look doubtful, carry a light weight travel towel of viscose material to do the job.

15. Use A Compression Bag

Compression bags are getting lots of recommendation now days from regular travellers. These are useful for saving space in your luggage when you have to pack bulky dresses. While packing for the return trip, get help from the hotel staff to arrange a vacuum cleaner.

Footwear

16. Put On Your Hiking Boots

If you have plans to go hiking or trekking during your trip, you will need those bulky hiking boots. The best way to carry them is to wear them on flight to save space and luggage weight. You can remove the boots once inside and be comfortable in your socks.

17. Picking The Right Shoes

Shoes are often the bulkiest items, along with being the dainty if you are a female. They need care and take up a lot of space in your luggage. It is advisable therefore to pick shoes very carefully. If you plan to do a lot of walking and site seeing, then wearing a pair of comfortable walking shoes are a must. For more formal occasions you can carry durable, light weight flats which will not take up much space.

18. Stuff Shoes

If you happen to pack a pair of shoes, ensure you utilize their hollow insides. Tuck small items like rolled up socks or belts to save space. They will also be easy to find.

Toiletries
19. Stashing Toiletries

Carry only absolute necessities. Airline rules dictate that for one carry-on bag, liquids and gels must be in 3.4 ounce (100ml) bottles or less, and must be packed in a one quart zip-lock bag. If you are planning to stay in a hotel, the basic things will be provided for you. It's best is to buy the rest from the local market at your destination.

20. Take Along Tampons

Tampons are a hard to find item in a lot of countries. Figure out how many you need and pack accordingly. For longer stays you can buy them online and have them delivered to where you are staying.

21. Get Pampered Before You Travel

Some avid travellers suggest getting a pedicure and manicure just the day before travelling. This not only gives you a well kept look, you also save the trouble of packing nail polish. Remember, every little bit of weight reduced adds up.

Electronics
22. Lugging Along Electronics

Electronics have a large role to play in our lives today. Most of us cannot imagine our lives away from our phones, laptops or tablets. However while travelling, one must consider the amount of weight these electronics add to our luggage. Thankfully smart phones come along with all the essentials tools like a camera, email access, picture editing tools and more. They are smart to the point of eliminating the need to carry multiple gadgets. Choose a smart phone that suits all your requirements and travel with the world in your palms or pocket.

23. Reduce the Number of Chargers

If you do travel with multiple electronic devices, you will have to bear the additional burden of carrying all their chargers too. Check if a single charger can be used for multiple devices. You might also consider investing in a pocket charger. These small devices support multiple devices while keeping you charged on the go.

24. Travel Friendly Apps

Along with smart phones come numerous apps, which are immensely helpful in our travels. You name it and you have an app for it at hand – take pictures, sharing with friends and family, torch to light dark roads, maps, checking flight/train times, find hotels and many other things. Use these smart alternatives to traditional items like books to eliminate weight and save space.

I get ideas about what's essential when packing my suitcase.

-Diane von Furstenberg

Travelling With Kids

25. Bring Along the Stroller

Kids might enjoy walking for a while but they soon tire out and a stroller is the just the right thing for them to rest in while you continue your tour. Strollers also double duty as a luggage carrier and shopping bag holder. Remember to pick a light weight, easy to handle brand of stroller. Better yet, find out in advance if you can rent a stroller at your destination.

26. Bring Only Enough Diapers for Your Trip

Diapers take up a lot of space and add to the weight of your luggage. Therefore it is advisable to carry just enough diapers to last through the trip and a few for afterwards, till you buy fresh stock at your destination. Unless of course you are travelling to a really remote area, in which case you have no choice but to carry the load. Otherwise diapers are something you will find pretty easily.

27. Take Only A Couple Of Toys

Children are easily attracted by new things in their environment. While travelling they will find numerous 'new' objects to scrutinize and play with. Packing just one favorite toy is enough, or if there is no favorite toy leave out all of them in favor of stories or imaginary games.

28. Carry Kid Friendly Snacks

Create a small snack counter in your bag to store away quick bites for those sudden hunger pangs. Depending on the child's age this could include chocolates, raisins, dry fruits, granola bars or biscuits. Also keep a bottle of water handy for your little one. These things do not add much weight and can be adjusted in a handbag or knapsack.

29. Games to Carry

Create some travel specific, imaginary games if you have slightly grown up children, like spot the attractions. Keep a coloring book and colors handy for in-flight or hotel time. Apps on your smart phone can keep the children engaged with cartoons and story books. Older children are often entertained by games available on phones or tablets. This cuts the weight of luggage down while keeping the kids entertained.

30. Let the Kids Carry Their Load

A good thing is to start early sharing of responsibilities. Let your child pick a bag of his or her choice and pack it themselves. Keep tabs on what they are stuffing in their bags by asking if they will be using that item on the trip. It could start out being just an entertainment bag initially but with growing years they will learn to sort the useful from the superfluous. Children as little as four can maneuver a small trolley suitcase like a pro- their experience in pull along toys credit. If you are worried that you may be pulling it for them, you may want to start with a backpack.

31. Decide on Location for Children to Sleep

While on a trip you might not always get a crib at your destination, and carrying one will make life all the more difficult. Instead call ahead to see if there are any cribs or roll out beds for children. You may even put blankets on the floor. Weave them a story about camping and they will gladly sleep without any trouble.

32. Get Baby Products Delivered At Your Destination

If you are absolutely paranoid about not getting your favourite variety of diaper or brand of baby food, check out online stores like amazon.com for services in your destination city. You can buy things online ahead of your travel and get them delivered to your hotel upon arrival.

33. Feeding Needs Of Your Infants

If you are travelling with a breastfed infant, you save the trouble of carrying bottles and bottle sanitization kits. For special food, or medications, you may need to call ahead to make sure you have a refrigerator where you are staying.

34. Feeding Needs of Your Toddler

With the progression from infancy to toddler, their dietary requirements too evolve. You will have to pack some snacks for travelling time. Fresh fruits and vegetables can be purchased at your destination. Most of the cities you travel to in whichever part of the world, will have baby food products and formulas, available at the local drug-store or the supermarket.

35. Picking Clothes for Your Baby

Contrary to popular belief, babies can do without many changes of clothes. At the most pack 2 outfits per day. Pack mix and match type clothes for your little one as well. Pick things which are comfortable to wear and quick to dry.

36. Selecting Shoes for Your Baby

Like outfits, kids can make do with two pairs of comfortable shoes. If you can get some water resistant shoes it will be best. To expedite drying wet shoes, you can stuff newspaper in them then wrap them with newspaper and leave them to dry overnight.

37. Keep One Change of Clothes Handy

Travelling with kids can be tricky. Keep a change of clothes for the kids and mum handy in your purse or tote bag. This takes a bit of space in your hand luggage but comes extremely handy in case there are any accidents or spills.

38. Leave Behind Baby Accessories

Baby accessories like their bed, bath tub, car seat, crib etc. should be left at home. Many hotels provide a crib on request, while car seats can be borrowed from friends or rented. Babies can be given a bath in the hotel sink or even in the adult bath tub with a little bit of water. If you bring a few bath toys, they can be used in the bath, pool, and out of water. They can also be sanitized easily in the sink.

39. Carry a Small Load Of Plastic Bags

With children around there are chances of a number of soiled clothes and diapers. These plastic bags help to sort the dirt from the clean inside your big bag. These are very light weight and come in handy to other carry stuff as well at times.

Pack with a Purpose

40. Packing for Business Trips

One neutral-colored suit should suffice. It can be paired with different shirts, ties and accessories for different occasions. One pair of black suit pants could be worn with a matching jacket for the office or with a snazzy top for dinner.

41. Packing for A Cruise

Most cruises have formal dinners, and that formal dress usually takes up a lot of space. However you might find a tuxedo to rent. For women, a short black dress with multiple accessory options will do the trick.

42. Packing for A Long Trip Over Different Climates

The secret packing mantra for travel over multiple climates is layering. Layering traps air around your body creating insulation against the cold. The same light t-shirt that is comfortable in a warmer climate can be the innermost layer in a colder climate.

Reduce Some More Weight

43. Leave Precious Things At Home

Things that you would hate to lose or get damaged leave them at home. Precious jewelry, expensive gadgets or dresses, could be anything. You will not require these on your trip. Leave them at home and spare the load on your mind.

44. Send Souvenirs by Mail

If you have spent all your money on purchasing souvenirs, carrying them back in the same bag that you brought along would be difficult. Either pack everything in another bag and check it in the airport or get everything shipped to your home. Use an international carrier for a secure transit, but this could be more expensive than the checking fees at the airport.

45. Avoid Carrying Books

Books equal to weight. There are many reading apps which you can download on your smart phone or tab. Plus there are gadgets like Kindle and Nook that are thinner and lighter alternatives to your regular book.

Check, Get, Set, Check Again

46. Strategize Before Packing

Create a travel list and prepare all that you think you need to carry along. Keep everything on your bed or floor before packing and then think through once again – do I really need that? Any item that meets this question can be avoided. Remove whatever you don't really need and pack the rest.

47. Test Your Luggage

Once you have fully packed for the trip take a test trip with your luggage. Take your bags and go to town for window shopping for an hour. If you enjoy your hour long trip it is good to go, if not, go home and reduce the load some more. Repeat this test till you hit the right weight.

48. Add a Roll Of Duct Tape

You might wonder why, when this book has been talking about reducing stuff, we're suddenly asking you to pack something totally unusual. This is because when you have limited supplies, duct tape is immensely helpful for small repairs – a broken bag, leaking zip-lock bag, broken sunglasses, you name it and duct tape can fix it, temporarily.

49. List of Essential Items

Even though the emphasis is on packing light, there are things which have to be carried for any trip. Here is our list of essentials:

- Passport/Visa or any other ID

- Any other paper work that might be required on a trip like permits, hotel reservation confirmations etc.

- Medicines – all your prescription medicines and emergency kit, especially if you are travelling with children

Mandy Herrington

- Medical or vaccination records
- Money in foreign currency if travelling to a different country
- Tickets- Email or Message them to your phone

50. Make the Most of Your Trip

Wherever you are going, whatever you hope to do we encourage you to embrace it whole-heartedly. Take in the scenery, the culture and above all, enjoy your time away from home.

On a long journey even a straw weighs heavy.

-Spanish Proverb

Packing and Planning Tips

A Week before Leaving

- Arrange for someone to take care of pets and water plants
- •Stop mail and newspaper
- Notify Credit Card companies where you are going.
- Change your thermostat settings
- Car inspected, oil is changed, and tires have the correct pressure.
- Passports and id is up to date.
- Pay bills.
- Copy important items and download travel Apps.
- Start collecting small bills for tips

Right Before Leaving

- Clean out refrigerator.
- Empty garbage cans.
- Lock windows.
- Make sure you have the right ID with you.
- Bring cash for tips.
- Remember travel documents.
- Lock door behind you.
- Remember wallet.
- Unplug items in house and pack chargers.

Mandy Herrington

Read other Greater Than a Tourist Books

Greater Than a Tourist San Miguel de Allende Guanajuato Mexico: 50 Travel Tips from a Local by Tom Peterson

Greater Than a Tourist – Lake George Area New York USA: 50 Travel Tips from a Local by Janine Hirschklau

Greater Than a Tourist – Monterey California United States: 50 Travel Tips from a Local by Katie Begley

Greater Than a Tourist – Chanai Crete Greece: 50 Travel Tips from a Local by Dimitra Papagrigoraki

Greater Than a Tourist – The Garden Route Western Cape Province South Africa: 50 Travel Tips from a Local by Li-Anne McGregor van Aardt

Greater Than a Tourist – Sevilla Andalusia Spain: 50 Travel Tips from a Local by Gabi Gazon

Greater Than a Tourist – Kota Bharu Kelantan Malaysia: 50 Travel Tips from a Local by Aditi Shukla

Children's Book: Charlie the Cavalier Travels the World by Lisa Rusczyk

Mandy Herrington

> TOURIST

Visit Greater Than a Tourist for Free Travel Tips
http://GreaterThanATourist.com

Sign up for the Greater Than a Tourist Newsletter for discount days, new books, and travel information:
http://eepurl.com/cxspyf

Follow us on Facebook for tips, images, and ideas:
https://www.facebook.com/GreaterThanATourist

Follow us on Pinterest for travel tips and ideas:
http://pinterest.com/GreaterThanATourist

Follow us on Instagram for beautiful travel images:
http://Instagram.com/GreaterThanATourist

Mandy Herrington

> TOURIST

Please leave your honest review of this book on Amazon and Goodreads. Please send your feedback to GreaterThanaTourist@gmail.com as we continue to improve the series. Thank you. We appreciate your positive and constructive feedback. Thank you.

Mandy Herrington

NOTES

Made in the USA
Las Vegas, NV
23 January 2023

66142507R00056